AMY K. DARLEY

THE EASY

KETO

CHRISTMAS COOKIE COOKBOOK

AN EASY BIY RECIPE GUIDE

FOR THE HOLIDAYS

CHEWY CHOCOLATE CHIP COOKIES

To many, chocolate chip cookies are one of the best types of cookies around. If you prefer a chewy cookie to a crunchy one, you will love the cookies made following the below recipe. The secret behind their chewiness is the brown sugar, a cookie miracle that increases the cookie's moisture content.

With this recipe, one can approximately bake two dozen medium-sized cookies.

INGREDIENTS
- 1 cup white sugar (202 grams)
- ⅓ cup brown sugar (73 grams)
- ½ teaspoon salt

- 1 egg (a decreasing egg yolk amount gives optimized lightness and fluffy texture to the dough)
- A cup of butter (between refrigerator and room temperature) (227g/8oz)
- ¼ cups (289 grams) of flour
- One teaspoon of baking soda
- teaspoon vanilla extract
- 2-3 tablespoons milk
- 2 cups of chocolate chips (if small or less if opposite).

PREPARATION

STEP 1

Preheat the oven to 180°C.

STEP 2

Add the vanilla, egg, sugar, brown sugar, and butter to a bowl.

STEP 3

Use coarser sugar to get thicker, chewier cookies. Dissolved sugar acts as a tenderizer interfering with dough structure, increasing spread because finer sugar dissolves more easily than coarser sugar. So if you prefer your cookies to keep their thick and chewy nature, use coarse sugar (or use finer sugar for the opposite effect). Should you decide to use powdered sugar for extra crispiness, be sure it doesn't have corn starch in it. Else you'll get unexpected results. Mix all ingredients until creamy texture.

STEP 4

Whisk flour, baking soda, and salt into a different bowl.

STEP 5

Mix dry and wet ingredients until thoroughly blended without over-mixing. Add the milk for a smoothly blended dough. Clumps of flour or lumps of butter are not allowed. Be sure all the ingredients are distributed evenly through your dough. After mixing, add the chocolate chips. Mix them in.

STEP 6

Rub cooking spray to a pan so that the cookies don't stick to the baking pan. Alternatively, use wax paper to line the pan.

STEP 7

Using your hands, roll a small quantity of your cookie dough into ball shapes. Because the balls flatten when baked, try visualizing your finished cookie's size as you form the balls of dough. Make 24 balls of dough.

STEP 8

Carefully place the cookie balls on the baking pan.

STEP 9

With a fork, flatten each cookie dough ball, and this will give distinct ridges and flatten the cookie neatly.

STEP 10

Put cookies in the oven for about 9-10 minutes. No overcooking, as they will continue to cook for a short while after you remove them from the oven.

STEP 11

Remove cookies from the oven, place them on a wire cooling rack for about 14- 15 minutes to cool. Use a spatula to avoid burning yourself on the melted chips when transferring the cookies to the rack. The cookies are ready to eat after the chocolate chips solidify again. Keep safe in an airtight container and enjoy with a chilled drink or ice cream.

AMY K. DARLEY

NO-BAKE CHOCOLATE OATMEAL COOKIES

Need to make a quick batch of cookies? Cool here is a recipe to make a batch of cookies with 40 minutes of prep time. Once they cool and all set, you will have a tasty treat for yourself.

INGREDIENTS

- 1/2 cup of butter or margarine
- 1/2 cup (120 ml) milk
- 2 cups (400 g) sugar
- 1/2 cup (60 g) cocoa
- 2 tsp. (10 ml) vanilla extract
- 1/2 cup (130 g) peanut butter (optional)
- 3 cups (245 g) of quick-cooking oats.

PREPARATION

STEP 1

Get a baking sheet lined with parchment paper, then set it aside.

STEP 2

Combine the butter or margarine, 1/2 cup of milk, 2 cups sugar, and 1/2 cup cocoa in a sizeable three-quart saucepan.

STEP 3

Place the pan over a medium heat source and stir the ingredients constantly until the mixture attains to a full rolling boil.

STEP 4

Boil the mixture for precisely one minute and then remove it from the heat. Timing is crucial in this recipe.

STEP 5

Stir in 3 cups of quick/minute oats, 2 teaspoons of vanilla extract, and 1/2 cup of peanut butter (optional). Mix everything well.

STEP 6

Place spoonfuls of the ready batter on the cookie sheet.

STEP 7

Put the cookies in a Refrigerator for 90 minutes to an hour before serving.

14

BANANA CHOCOLATE CHIP COOKIES.

This soft cookie has a taste of banana bread and a chocolate chip cookie simultaneously. Loved by all, especially kids! Read through to learn how to make banana chocolate chip cookies. (Makes about 18 cookies)

INGREDIENTS

- 2 cups (316g) all-purpose flour
- 1 tsp. baking powder
- 1/2 tsp. salt
- 1/4 tsp. baking soda
- 1/2 cup (102g) white sugar
- 1/2 cup (109g) brown sugar
- 2/3 cup (151g) butter, softened
- 2 Eggs

- 1 tsp. vanilla extract
- 1/2 cups bananas, mashed
- 2 cups (335g) semisweet chocolate chips.

UTENSILS

Large bowl

Medium bowl

Wooden spoon

Parchment paper

Cookie sheet

Hand mixer

PREPARATION

STEP 1

Preheat the oven to 200°C.

STEP 2

Sift and mix the flour, salt, baking powder, and baking soda in a medium bowl.

STEP 3

Use a mixer to get the sugars and butter creamy in a large bowl.

STEP 4

Thoroughly combine the eggs, vanilla, and mashed bananas in the butter mixture.

STEP 5

Gently but steadily pour the flour mixture into the butter mixture. Mix thoroughly with a (wooden) spoon, and lastly, add the chocolate chips.

STEP 6

On a pre-greased or Parchment paper layered cookie sheet, Place spoonfuls of the dough.

STEP 7

Bake the cookies for about 10 to 13 minutes.

STEP 8

Cool completely on a cooling rack. And enjoy your chilled drink.

CHOCOLATE CHIP SNOWBALL COOKIES

Sure, you have heard of a traditional butter cookie made with nuts and powdered sugar. Here is how it's done.

INGREDIENTS

- 170g of butter, softened
- 100g of sugar
- 1/2 teaspoon of salt
- 1 large egg
- 2 teaspoons of vanilla extract
- 240g of all-purpose flour
- 125g of chopped pecans or walnuts
- 176g of mini-chocolate chips
- Powdered sugar for rolling the cookies.

20

PREPARATION

STEP 1

Switch on the oven and prepare your work stations. Preheat the oven to a temperature of about 170 degrees. Set aside a few baking sheets. You'll also need wire racks set up for cooling the baked cookies. Get out your mixing bowls as well as measuring cups. Let 171 g of butter come to room temperature.

Needless greasing the baking sheets for this recipe as the cookie dough already contains enough butter. The done cookies should come off of the baking pan quite easily.

STEP 2

Get the butter, sugar, and salt creamy. Put the softened butter in a large mixing bowl and add 100 g of sugar and 1/2 teaspoon salt. Continue beating the mixture at medium speed until it turns fluffy. Take your time.

Getting the butter and sugar creamy will create volume. Since these cookies don't have any leavening agent (like baking soda or baking powder), it's crucial to beat the butter and sugar until they're light.

STEP 3

Stir in the egg and vanilla extract. Pause the mixer and add one large egg and 2-3 teaspoons of vanilla extract to the mixing bowl. Set the mixer on low speed and beat the dough until all ingredients are thoroughly combined.

Avoid mixing in the egg at high speed, as this could cause the egg to fly out of the mixing bowl.

STEP 4

Add the flour, pecans, and mini-chocolate chips. Keep the mixer at low speed and slowly pour in 2 cups of all-purpose flour. Pour in 1 cup of chopped pecans or walnuts and 1 cup of mini-chocolate chips and stir the dough until the nuts and chocolate are blended.

You can either refrigerate the dough at this point or shape it into balls for baking.

Should you instead not want noticeable chunks of nuts in your cookies, you can grind them to a fine texture in a food processor.

STEP 5 (SHAPE THE COOKIES)

Scoop the cookie dough into small (2.5 cm) balls. Gently roll them to perfectly round shapes between your palms and set them on the ungreased baking sheets.

Ensure that the cookies are placed at least 2 cm apart from each other on the sheets to provide them with space for expansion as they cook.

STEP 6

Bake the snowball cookies. Place the cookie doughs in the preheated oven and bake them for about 20 minutes.

The baked cookies will not turn very dark or golden, but the bottom will have a light brown color when they are done baking. You should be able to perceive the aroma once the cookies are done. Bring out the sheets from the oven and let the cookies rest for 3 minutes.

Don't worry about the pale look; this will give them more snowballs look.

STEP 7

Roll the cookies in powdered sugar, and once they are cool enough to handle, roll them in a

dish of powdered sugar. Each cookie should be wholly coated to have the snowball look. Set the cookies to finish cooling.

This recipe makes approximately 4 dozen chocolate chip snowball cookies.

STEP 8

Store in a dry airtight container.

CHOCOLATE CHIP PEANUT BUTTER COOKIES

The lovely taste of chocolate and peanuts have always been fused in fudges, candies, and cupcakes, but not as many cookies. Here is how to make a classic one. The recipe makes about 43 cookies.

INGREDIENTS
- 3 cups of flour
- 1/4 teaspoon salt
- 1/2 teaspoon baking soda
- 1 1/2 cups brown sugar
- 1 cup of butter
- 1 cup of white sugar
- 2 eggs
- 2 teaspoons of vanilla extract

- 1 cup of peanut butter
- 2 cups of semisweet chocolate chips.

PREPARATION

STEP 1

Preheat the oven to 164 °c.

STEP 2

Pour in the dry ingredients (flour, baking soda, and salt) in a bowl, mix well with a whisk and put aside.

STEP 3

Mix brown and white sugar in an electric mixer. Add the vanilla extract, butter, and eggs to the mixture and mix till fluffy.

STEP 4

Pour the flour mixture, chocolate chips, and peanut butter into the cross, and mix thoroughly with an electric mixer.

STEP 5

Set a well-greased cookie sheet and Place spoonfuls of the dough on it. Ensure adequate spacing between them, Bake for 20 minutes or until light brown color. When done, transfer them to a much cooler surface to cool off.

STEP 6

Finished. Store in an airtight container.

FREE TIP

Use the right sizes for everything. For the flour mixture, use a medium bowl, and for the butter mixture, use a large bowl.

29

AMY K. DARLEY

CHOCOLATE CHIP COOKIE DOUGH CHEESECAKE

Who doesn't like cheesecake? And who wants to bake some?

INGREDIENTS

- 60g of finely crushed chocolate wafer cookies
- 1 cup (200 grams) of sugar
- 1/4 cup (60 grams) of melted butter
- 230 grams of cream cheese, diced
- 2 cups (460 grams) of sour cream
- 3 eggs
- 2 teaspoons of vanilla extract
- 1/4 cup (60 grams) of butter
- 1/4 cup (55 grams) of packed brown sugar

- 1/4 cup (45 grams) of white sugar
- 2 tablespoons water
- 1 teaspoon of vanilla extract
- 1/2 cup (61 grams) of all-purpose flour
- 1 cup (170 grams) of semisweet chocolate chips
- 2 teaspoons (10 grams) of white sugar.

PREPARATION

STEP 1

Preheat oven to 180 degrees.

STEP 2

Mix the chocolate wafer cookie crumbs, 2 tablespoons of white sugar, and the melted butter. Press hard into the bottom of a baking pan and bake for 8 minutes.

STEP 3

Now make the cookie dough:

In a bowl, beat 1/3 cup butter or margarine with the brown sugar and 1/3 cup of the white sugar; add 1 teaspoon of the vanilla.

Pour in the flour and the semisweet chocolate chips. Stir until well combined.

STEP 4

(MAKING THE CHEESECAKE)

In a food processor or blender, whisk 1 cup white sugar and all of the cream cheese.

Add 1 cup of sour cream, eggs, and 1 teaspoon of vanilla.

Mix all ingredients well, then pour into the already prepared crust.

STEP 5

Let the cookie dough fall evenly over the cake in 2 tablespoons and slide the dough below the surface. Baking should last for 37-40 minutes at 340 degrees F. The cake will shake gently in the middle. Spread the filling on the hot cake. Let the cake cool, then refrigerate in the refrigerator for at least 4 hours until cold.

STEP 6

For the filling: Stir in 1 cup of the remaining sour cream, 1 teaspoon of vanilla, and 2 teaspoons of white sugar until smooth. Spread on a hot cake.

STEP 7

Store in a dry, tightly closed box.

FREE TIP

Put a pot of hot water in the oven with your cheesecake to provide moisture and prevent the cheesecake from cracking.

HOMEMADE OREO COOKIES

Oreos are a classic favorite; I bet you didn't know you could make them at home? Homemade Oreos don't exactly taste the same as what you'll find in the store, but they're delicious. With a few basic baking ingredients and a simple buttercream frosting, you can make your homemade Oreo whenever you want!

INGREDIENTS
- Biscuits
- 3 cups of flour
- 3/4 cup of cocoa powder
- 1 teaspoon of baking powder
- 1/4 teaspoon of salt
- 1/4 teaspoon of baking powder

- 3 sticks of butter (softened)
- 2 cups of sugar 2 eggs
- additional granulated sugar for the cookie dough filling icing
- 2 sticks of butter (softened)
- 2 cups of caster sugar (powdered sugar)
- 1 tablespoon of vanilla extract.

PREPARATION

STEP 1

Preheat the oven to 177 ° C. Your oven should be hot when you put the cookies. So heat it just before you start making your cookie dough. This way, you make sure it's ready to use when you're ready to bake your cookies.

STEP 2

Except for sugar, mix other dry ingredients in a large bowl. Add the flour, cocoa powder, baking powder, salt, and baking powder to one large mixing bowl, take a spoon or a whisk and mix the dry ingredients in the bowl until they are combined.

STEP 3

Combine butter and sugar in a dry mixing bowl. In another bowl, add the three sticks of butter and the two cups of sugar. Then beat the ingredients at medium speed with your kitchen mixer or hand mixer until everything is well combined.

STEP 4

Add the eggs. Once the butter and sugar are all mixed, add the eggs and mix them with the butter and sugar until well combined. Use your hand mixer or kitchen mixer to mix everything.

If you don't want to use eggs, you can always substitute the eggs with an egg substitute like Ener-G or ground flaxseeds.

STEP 5

Pour in the dry ingredients while the blender is running. Then you need to add the dry ingredients to the mixture of butter, sugar, and eggs using the hand mixer. Slowly add the dry ingredients.

Keep the hand mixer or stand mixer at low to medium speed to prevent dry ingredients from escaping.

STEP 6

Line a cookie pan with parchment paper, so the cookie dough doesn't stick to your pan, cover the cake pan with a sheet of parchment paper, even if the pan has a non-stick coating. Cover the entire surface with a sheet of parchment paper.

If you don't have parchment paper, spray the pan with a non-stick coating. You can also use a small quantity of butter or oil if you don't have non-stick cooking spray.

STEP 7

Put the dough on baking paper. Use a small ice cream scoop or melon balls to scoop out about a tablespoon of cookie dough and place it on the pan. Leave about 5 cm between each ball and make sure the cookie balls are evenly distributed. If you want more even cakes, you can flatten all the dough on a clean surface and then use a cake cutter or cake cutter to cut out dough slices. Sprinkle flour over the body and the dough to keep it from sticking.

STEP 8

Flatten the balls on the cookie dough. Flattening the cookies makes them easier to use for sandwiches and gives the cookies an Oreo-like appearance. To do this, you need a clean drinking glass and a bowl of powdered sugar.

To flatten the cookie dough balls, take a clean drinking glass and push it into one of the cookies to flatten it.

Then peel the cookie and press the glass bottom with the powdered sugar into the bowl.

Squeeze the sugar onto the cake you just flattened. Repeat the above process for individual cookies.

STEP 9

Bake the cakes for 15 to 17 minutes. When your cakes are flat, place the tray in the preheated oven and set a timer for 15 or 17 minutes. If you bake the cakes for 15 minutes, you will get hard cakes. If you bake them for 17 minutes, they will turn into crispy cakes.

STEP 10

(MAKE THE ICING)

Butter and powdered sugar are the main ingredients in your frosting, so Place both in a large mixing bowl.

For easy frosting, keep butter at room temperature.

You can use vegetable fat as a substitute for some or all of the butter if you want.

STEP 11

Using a hand mixer to blend the butter and sugar. Set your hand mixer or kitchen mixer on low to combine the butter and powdered sugar. If you put it faster, some of the sugar may fly out of the bowl. Therefore, slow speed is preferable. Mix the butter and sugar to smoothness and fluffiness.

You can increase the speed a bit once the ingredients are well combined, but you can always keep it low to avoid splashing.

STEP 12

Pour 1 tablespoon of vanilla extract. When the butter and sugar are well mixed, it's time to add the vanilla extract. Pour the vanilla extract over the butter and sugar and remix the ingredients using your hand mixer or food processor. Mix the vanilla from low to medium speed.

Keep mixing the ingredients until the frosting is loose.

You may want to stop once or twice to scrape the sides of the bowl.

If you want a different flavor for your frosting, just replace another extract with vanilla. For example, if you want, you can use almond extract, chocolate extract, or caramel extract.

STEP 13

(PUT THE COOKIES TOGETHER)

Wait for the cookies to cool. When the cakes are made, take them out of the oven and place them on a cooling rack. Wait for the baked cakes to completely cool before doing something, or the icing will melt.

First, try baking the cakes, placing them on the rack to cool, and then starting the frosting. When you are done frosting, the cakes should be cool.

STEP 14

Put a tablespoon of frosting on each cake. Once the cakes have cooled, you can start adding the frosting topping. Use a small ice cream scoop or melon scoop to scoop up a tablespoon of frosting in the middle of half of your cookies.

Don't worry about smearing or hitting the enamel. Soup the scoops of ice cream on top of the cake.

Put another cookie on top of the frosting. Then you need to put a new cookie on the frozen cookies and press the two cookies together. This means the frosting can be spread and evenly distributed over the cake.

Please do this for all your cookies until they are all compressed.

STEP 15

Enjoy your homemade Oreo! Once you've squeezed your cookies, they're ready to eat! To be enjoyed alone or with a glass of milk.

If you don't plan on serving the cakes right away, you can put them in the refrigerator to prevent the icing from melting.

CHOCOLATE CAKE

After making this chocolate chip dough, drop the cookies on a baking sheet with a cake spoon or tablespoon. The coffee in the icing helps bring out the flavor of the chocolate.

INGREDIENTS

- Biscuits
- 1 slice of butter, room temperature
- 1 cup of packed brown sugar
- 1 egg
- 1/2 cup milk, room temperature
- 1 teaspoon of vanilla extract
- 56g of unsweetened chocolate, melted and cooled
- 1 cup of whole wheat flour
- 1/2 teaspoon of yeast
- 1/2 teaspoon of kosher salt
- 1/2 cup of chopped walnuts (optional).

ICING

- 2 cups of confectionery sugar
- 1/4 cup of unsweetened cocoa
- 1/2 pat of butter, room temperature
- 1/4 cup of strongly brewed coffee, hot
- 3/4 tsp. of Vanilla extract

PREPARATION
(BAKE THE CAKES)

If possible, do not melt your chocolate in the microwave as the temperature will be too high, and the chocolate can burn quickly. Instead, melt the chocolate in a double boiler on the stove.

STEP 1

Preheat the oven to 180 ° C and place a baking sheet with baking paper.

STEP 2

Put both butter and brown sugar in a large mixing bowl. Using a hand mixer or a kitchen mixer with a paddle, beat the butter and sugar until the ingredients are light and fluffy. Your blender should be at medium speed.

STEP 3

Stir in eggs, milk, vanilla, and refrigerated melted chocolate until ingredients are combined.

STEP 4

Combine the dry ingredients (salt, baking powder, and flour) in another mixing bowl with a whisk.

STEP 5

Pour bits of the dry ingredients into the wet ingredients and mix on low speed.

STEP 6

Once the first batch of dry ingredients has been mixed, add another third.

STEP 7

Gradually add the dry ingredients until they are mixed with the wet ingredients, but do not heat the dough.

STEP 8

When using, blend the nuts with a flat plastic spatula.

STEP 9

Use a cookie or a tablespoon to place the cookies on the baking sheet. Place cookies 5 inches apart so they can spread out while baking.

48

STEP 10

Bake the cakes for 8-10 minutes.

STEP 11

Take the baking sheet out of the oven and let the cakes cool on the baking sheet for 2 minutes.

STEP 12

Use a spatula to move the cookies around the wire rack to cool completely.

STEP 13 (ADD ICING)

Please make sure the cookies are completely cool before freezing them, so the frosting does not melt when you roll them out.

In a clean mixing bowl, whisk together powdered sugar, cocoa powder, butter, coffee, and vanilla. You can use the regular hand mixer or a stand mixer with a paddle.

STEP 14

Use a cheese shaker or a butter knife to spread the frost over the cooled cake.

STEP 15

Serve the cakes with a glass of cold milk.

OATMEAL COOKIES

Oatmeal cookies are famous chew pies that anyone can make, and nothing beats a hot, perfectly flavored oatmeal pie. Best served hot. You'd be hard-pressed to keep enough for the cake bowl!

INGREDIENTS
- 1 cup of butter
- 1 cup of brown sugar
- 1.5 cups of sugar
- 2 Egg
- 1.5 cups of flour
- 1 teaspoon of baking powder
- 1 teaspoon of salt
- 1 teaspoon of cinnamon
- 3 cups of Quaker oats (no instant)
- 1 to 1-1 / 2 cups raisins

If you wish to add a slightly richer flavor, add a teaspoon of hot milk to the bowl while stirring. These are the two methods of preparations:

PREPARATION (METHOD 1)

STEP 1

Preheat the oven to 350 ° F. Fill the baking sheet with parchment paper or spray with non-stick cooking spray to ensure the cookies stay clean.

STEP 2

Mix the butter and sugar by hand. Place the white sugar, butter, and brown sugar in a mixing bowl at room temperature and slowly increase your blender's speed. You want everything to be mixed up and the mixture to be light and chewy.

STEP 3

Add and mix the eggs and vanilla until well blended. Work slowly through the eggs at first to avoid splashing water. Add the vanilla and mix until everything is smooth and the same color.

STEP 4

Beat the flour, baking powder, cinnamon, and salt in another bowl. You want all the dry ingredients to be evenly distributed before you add them. Use a fork or a small whisk to break up any lumps, which will make the dough much smoother and easier to work with while baking.

STEP 5

Slowly mix the flour mixture with the butter mixture. Gradually add flour in 3-4 parts, mixing each piece separately. Don't let all the flour get in and turn on the mixer - much more ends up on the counter than in the cake. Stir until all the flour is incorporated into the mixture and there is nothing on the sides of the bowl.

STEP 6

Stir in the raisins and oats with a rubber spatula. Stop using the hand mixer if all the flour is in it. The flour hardens the more you beat it, resulting in denser, less chewy cakes. Add the oats and raisins and mix with the spatula. Stop once dispersed.

STEP 7

Place round balls on your lined or greased baking sheet. You can roll them into balls to make perfect cakes, but this is rarely necessary. Scrape 1 to 2 tablespoons of the dough and place it on the cake. Provide enough space between cookies.

Whatever size you choose for your cakes, keep them consistent across all cakes to bake for the same amount of time.

STEP 8

Bake for 12 minutes, until golden brown but still tender. There should be small wet cracks on the top of the cake, which harden slightly as it cools if you take them out

 Once they've completely hardened, you'll be left with some crispy cookies.

STEP 9

Cool the cookies on a wire rack on the tray for 1 to 2 minutes, then transfer them to a wire rack and serve. Wire racks allow the whole cookie to cool at the same speed, resulting in better consistency and toughness.

METHOD 2

STEP 1

Add a little more than raisins to the dough. Take a cup of raisins from the original recipe and cut it in half. Find out what to replace it with. The following options all work well for raisins, but you can just as easily replace all of those raisins with these ingredients if you want:

Chocolate chips or pieces (white and dark chocolate work particularly well)

Chopped nuts, pecans, or almonds

Dried cranberries

STEP 2

Add 2 tablespoons of molasses and remove the equivalent amount of brown sugar for a spicy maple flavor. This thick, creamy, dark syrup pairs beautifully with the spicy flavors of a delicious oatmeal cake.

STEP 3

Season your cakes with a refreshing blend of chai spices. This fantastic cake takes all the joy with a good raisin and oatmeal cake and blows it with a fresh, tasty, and always delicious burst of sweet Indian spices. Add the following herbs and when you are feeling culinary, soak the raisins in a cup of chai tea for 15 minutes:

1 teaspoon of cardamom, cinnamon, ground cloves, 1/2 teaspoon of ginger, nutmeg, 1/4 teaspoon of ground black pepper.

STEP 4

Add 1 tablespoon of vanilla salt or triple the salt in the recipe and add dark chocolate for an incredibly subtle treat. Both sweet and savory, the addition of vanilla salt, often sold under the name "Vanilla Fleur de Sel" brings out a richness and a slightly salty taste that transform cakes from a simple dessert to a snack.

STEP 5

Consider adding a cup of grated coconut instead of a cup of oats. The texture remains pretty much the same, but you get a sweet, slightly tropical touch of coconut flavor that will surprise all guests. You can add as much or as little as you want, although at least 1 1/2 cups of oats is best to keep the cakes in their shape.

STEP 6

Make vegan oatmeal raisins by replacing the butter with flaxseed, almond butter, and applesauce. You don't need the hand mixer and can hand mix instead. Add the following ingredients and mix into a paste. Then mix everything else as usual:

- 1/2 cup applesauce
- 4 tablespoons of almond butter
- 4 tablespoons of ground flax seeds.

Enjoy your delicious cake.

AMY K. DARLEY

ENJOY YOUR HOLIDAYS